Super Easy
AIR FRYER

pil
Publications International, Ltd.

Copyright © 2026 Publications International, Ltd.
All rights reserved. This publication may not be reproduced or quoted in whole or in part by any means whatsoever without written permission from:

Louis Weber, CEO
Publications International, Ltd.
5250 Old Orchard Road, Suite 500
Skokie, IL 60077

Permission is never granted for commercial purposes.

Photograph on front cover and page 33 copyright © Shutterstock.com.

Pictured on the front cover: Sweet and Spicy Wings *(page 32).*

Pictured on the back cover *(clockwise from top left):* Loaded Tater Tots *(page 20),* Easy Turkey Turnovers *(page 56),* California BBQ Burgers *(page 112),* Teriyaki Salmon *(page 132),* Mediterranean Gnocchi *(page 150),* Savory Garlic Mushrooms *(page 180)* and Eggplant Pizzas *(page 154).*

ISBN: 979-8-89746-144-8

Manufactured in China.

8 7 6 5 4 3 2 1

Microwave Cooking: Microwave ovens vary in wattage. Use the cooking times as guidelines and check for doneness before adding more time.

WARNING: Food preparation, baking and cooking involve inherent dangers: misuse of electric products, sharp electric tools, boiling water, hot stoves, allergic reactions, foodborne illnesses and the like, pose numerous potential risks. Publications International, Ltd. (PIL) assumes no responsibility or liability for any damages you may experience as a result of following recipes, instructions, tips or advice in this publication.

While we hope this publication helps you find new ways to eat delicious foods, you may not always achieve the results desired due to variations in ingredients, cooking temperatures, typos, errors, omissions or individual cooking abilities.

Let's get social!

 @Publications_International

 @PublicationsInternational

www.pilbooks.com

Table of Contents

Appetizers and Snacks

PIGS IN BLANKETS

- 1 container (8 ounces) refrigerated crescent roll dough
- 1 package (about 12 ounces) cocktail franks
- Mustard (optional)

1. Unroll dough on cutting board or work surface; separate into eight triangles. Cut each triangle into three long, thin triangles.
2. Place one frank at base of each triangle; roll up dough toward opposite point.
3. Preheat air fryer to 330°F.
4. Cook franks in single layer 6 to 8 minutes or until golden brown. Serve with mustard, if desired.

MAKES 4 SERVINGS

POLENTA FRIES

- **1 roll (about 17 ounces) prepared polenta**
- **2 teaspoons olive oil**
- **¼ teaspoon salt**
- **2 tablespoons grated Parmesan cheese (optional)**
- **Ketchup, aioli or favorite dipping sauce (optional)**

1. Cut rounded ends off polenta roll. Cut roll in half crosswise; cut each half lengthwise into four slices. Cut each slice into four sticks (about 3×½ inch).
2. Preheat air fryer to 400°F. Brush both sides of polenta sticks with oil; sprinkle with salt.
3. Cook polenta in single layer 9 minutes; turn and cook 4 to 5 minutes or until crisp and edges are beginning to brown. Sprinkle with cheese; serve warm with ketchup, if desired.

MAKES 3 TO 4 SERVINGS

TIP: Add additional flavor to polenta fries by sprinkling them with garlic powder, Italian seasoning or smoked paprika after brushing them with oil.

CRISPY FRIED CAMEMBERT

- **1 round (about 7 ounces) Camembert cheese**
- **1 cup panko bread crumbs**
- **⅛ teaspoon salt**
- **⅛ teaspoon black pepper**
- **2 eggs**
- **Mixed greens, fruit jam or fruit chutney (optional)**

1. Cut Camembert into eight wedges. Line small baking sheet or plate with parchment paper or waxed paper.
2. Combine panko, ⅛ teaspoon salt and ⅛ teaspoon pepper in shallow dish. Beat eggs in another shallow dish; season with pinch of salt and pepper.
3. Dip cheese wedges in egg, letting excess drip back into dish. Roll in panko to coat. Dip again in egg and panko. Place on prepared baking sheet; freeze 30 minutes to 1 hour.
4. Preheat air fryer to 365°F. Line basket with parchment paper.
5. Place cheese wedges in single layer in basket; spray generously with nonstick cooking spray. Cook about 10 minutes or until golden brown, turning several times and spraying again with cooking spray. Serve with mixed greens, if desired.

MAKES 3 TO 4 SERVINGS

TOASTED TORTELLINI

- **2 eggs**
- **2 tablespoons milk**
- **⅔ cup Italian-seasoned bread crumbs**
- **2 tablespoons grated Parmesan cheese**
- **1 teaspoon garlic powder**
- **½ teaspoon salt**
- **1 package (9 ounces) refrigerated tortellini**
- **Chopped fresh parsley (optional)**
- **Marinara sauce**

1. Beat eggs and milk in shallow dish. Combine bread crumbs, cheese, garlic powder and salt in another shallow dish.
2. Dip tortellini in egg mixture, letting excess drip back into dish. Roll in bread crumb mixture to coat. Spray with nonstick cooking spray.
3. Preheat air fryer to 370°F. Spray basket with cooking spray.
4. Cook tortellini in single layer 6 to 8 minutes or until golden brown and crisp, shaking halfway through cooking. Sprinkle with parsley, if desired; serve with marinara sauce.

MAKES 6 TO 8 SERVINGS

CRUNCHY PARMESAN ZUCCHINI STICKS

- **1 package (3 ounces) ramen noodles, any flavor**
- **½ cup shredded Parmesan cheese**
- **½ cup all-purpose flour**
- **1 egg**
- **1 tablespoon water**
- **3 medium zucchini, cut into sticks**
- **Marinara sauce**

1 Combine noodles and cheese in food processor; pulse until crumbs form. Pour into shallow dish.

2 Combine flour and ramen seasoning packet in another shallow dish. Beat egg and water in third shallow dish.

3 Dip zucchini sticks in flour mixture, then in egg, then in noodle mixture, turning to coat. Spray with nonstick cooking spray.

4 Preheat air fryer to 390°F. Line basket with parchment paper; spray with cooking spray.

5 Cook zucchini in batches 8 to 10 minutes or until zucchini is tender and coating is golden brown. Serve warm with marinara sauce.

MAKES 6 SERVINGS

CRISPY MUSHROOMS

- ½ cup all-purpose flour
- ½ cup garlic- and herb-flavored bread crumbs
- ½ cup grated Parmesan cheese
- ½ teaspoon paprika
- ½ teaspoon salt
- ¼ teaspoon black pepper
- 2 eggs
- 1 teaspoon water
- 1 package (8 ounces) mushrooms, stems trimmed

GARLIC MAYONNAISE

- ½ cup mayonnaise
- 2 teaspoons minced garlic
- 1 teaspoon lemon juice

1. Combine flour, bread crumbs, cheese, paprika, salt and pepper in medium bowl. Beat eggs and water in another medium bowl.
2. Preheat air fryer to 370°F. Line basket with parchment paper.
3. Using fork, dip mushrooms in egg mixture, letting excess drip back into bowl. Dip in bread crumb mixture, turning to coat completely. Spray mushrooms with nonstick cooking spray.
4. Cook mushrooms in batches 6 to 8 minutes or until golden brown, shaking and spraying again halfway though cooking.
5. Meanwhile, combine mayonnaise, garlic and lemon juice in small bowl; mix well. Serve with mushrooms.

MAKES 4 SERVINGS

HONEY-GLAZED BISCUIT DOUGHNUTS

- **1 container (about 16 ounces) refrigerated jumbo biscuits (8 biscuits)**
- **¼ cup honey**
- **1 tablespoon chopped pistachio nuts**

1. Separate biscuits. Poke hole in center of each biscuit with fingers or handle of wooden spoon to create doughnut shape.
2. Preheat air fryer to 370°F.
3. Cook doughnuts in single layer 7 to 8 minutes or until golden brown.
4. Drizzle warm doughnuts with honey; sprinkle with pistachios. Serve immediately.

MAKES 8 DOUGHNUTS

VARIATION: For cinnamon-sugar coating, combine ¼ cup sugar and 1 teaspoon ground cinnamon in small bowl. Dip warm doughnuts in cinnamon-sugar.

MOZZARELLA STICKS

- ¼ cup all-purpose flour
- 2 eggs
- 1 tablespoon water
- 1 cup plain dry bread crumbs
- 2 teaspoons Italian seasoning
- ½ teaspoon salt
- ½ teaspoon garlic powder
- 1 package (12 ounces) string cheese (12 sticks)
- 1 cup marinara or pizza sauce

1. Place flour in shallow dish. Beat eggs and water in another shallow dish. Combine bread crumbs, Italian seasoning, salt and garlic powder in third shallow dish.
2. Coat each piece of cheese with flour. Dip in egg mixture, letting excess drip back into dish. Roll in bread crumb mixture to coat. Dip again in egg mixture and roll again in bread crumb mixture. Place on baking sheet. Refrigerate until ready to cook.
3. Preheat air fryer to 370°F. Line basket with parchment paper; spray with nonstick cooking spray.
4. Cook cheese sticks in batches 8 to 10 minutes or until golden brown, turning halfway through cooking. Serve with marinara sauce.

MAKES 6 SERVINGS

LOADED TATER TOTS

- **1 package (16 ounces) frozen bite-size potato nuggets (tater tots)**
- **½ cup (2 ounces) shredded Cheddar cheese**
- **2 slices bacon, crisp-cooked and crumbled* *or* 2 tablespoons bacon bits**
- **2 tablespoons sour cream**
- **2 green onions, chopped**
- **Chopped avocado (optional)**

Cook bacon in preheated 390°F air fryer 6 to 8 minutes or until crisp. Remove to paper towel-lined plate.

1. Preheat air fryer to 390°F.
2. Cook potatoes in single layer 6 to 8 minutes, shaking occasionally during cooking.
3. Transfer potatoes to baking dish that fits inside air fryer; sprinkle with cheese and bacon. Cook 2 to 3 minutes or until cheese is melted.
4. Drizzle with sour cream; sprinkle with green onions and avocado, if desired. Serve immediately.

MAKES 3 TO 4 SERVINGS

PEPPERONI PIZZA BAGELS

- **4 bagels, cut in half horizontally**
- **¼ cup marinara sauce**
- **¼ cup (1 ounce) shredded mozzarella cheese**
- **¼ cup mini pepperoni slices**
- **Dried oregano**

1. Top bagel halves with marinara sauce, cheese and pepperoni.
2. Preheat air fryer to 350°F. Line basket with foil or parchment paper.
3. Cook bagels 3 to 5 minutes or until cheese is melted and beginning to brown. Sprinkle with oregano.

MAKES 4 SERVINGS

GREEN BEAN DIPPERS

- 1 egg
- 1 pound green beans, ends trimmed
- ½ cup plain dry bread crumbs
- 2 tablespoons grated Parmesan cheese
- 1 tablespoon olive oil
- ½ teaspoon garlic powder
- ¼ teaspoon salt
- Ranch salad dressing (optional)

1. Beat egg in large bowl. Add green beans; toss to coat. Combine bread crumbs, cheese, oil, garlic powder and salt in small bowl; mix well.
2. Sprinkle bread crumb mixture over green beans; toss to coat.
3. Preheat air fryer to 390°F. Line basket with parchment paper.
4. Cook green beans in batches 8 to 10 minutes or until crisp, shaking occasionally during cooking. Serve with dressing, if desired.

MAKES 6 SERVINGS

AIR-FRIED BOWTIE BITES

- **8 ounces uncooked bowtie (farfalle) pasta or favorite shaped pasta (such as shells or tubes)**
- **1½ tablespoons olive oil**
- **¼ cup grated Parmesan cheese**
- **½ teaspoon salt**
- **½ teaspoon garlic powder**
- **¼ teaspoon black pepper**
- **Marinara sauce**

1. Prepare pasta according to package directions for al dente. Drain pasta (do not rinse); transfer to large bowl.
2. Preheat air fryer to 390°F.
3. Drizzle oil over pasta. Add cheese, salt, garlic powder and pepper; toss to coat.
4. Cook pasta in single layer 10 to 12 minutes or until lightly browned and crisp around edges, shaking occasionally during cooking. Season with additional salt and pepper, if desired. Serve with marinara sauce.

MAKES 8 TO 10 SERVINGS

SAVORY PITA CHIPS

2 whole wheat or white pita bread rounds

2 tablespoons grated Parmesan cheese

1 teaspoon dried basil

¼ teaspoon garlic powder

1. Split pita rounds in half horizontally; separate each into two rounds. Cut each round into six wedges; spray wedges with nonstick cooking spray.
2. Combine cheese, basil and garlic powder in small bowl; mix well. Sprinkle evenly over pita wedges.
3. Preheat air fryer to 350°F.
4. Cook pita wedges 8 to 10 minutes or until golden brown, shaking occasionally during cooking. Cool completely before serving.

MAKES 4 SERVINGS

CINNAMON CRISPS: Substitute butter-flavored cooking spray for nonstick cooking spray and 1 tablespoon sugar mixed with ¼ teaspoon ground cinnamon for the Parmesan, basil and garlic powder.

SPICY ROASTED CHICKPEAS

- **1 can (about 15 ounces) chickpeas, rinsed and drained**
- **1 tablespoon olive oil**
- **¼ teaspoon salt**
- **¼ teaspoon black pepper**
- **¼ tablespoon chili powder**
- **¼ teaspoon ground red pepper**
- **1 lime, cut into wedges (optional)**

1. Combine chickpeas, oil, salt and black pepper in large bowl; mix well.
2. Preheat air fryer to 390°F.
3. Cook chickpeas 8 to 10 minutes or until beginning to brown, shaking occasionally during cooking.
4. Sprinkle with chili powder and red pepper; stir to coat. Serve with lime wedges, if desired.

MAKES 1½ CUPS

NOTE: Roasted chickpeas can be eaten as a snack or used a topping for salads—they offer a healthy and flavorful alternative to croutons.

BAGEL CHIPS WITH EVERYTHING SEASONING DIP

- **2 large bagels, cut vertically into thin (¼-inch) slices**
- **1 container (12 ounces) whipped cream cheese**
- **1½ tablespoons finely chopped green onion**
- **1 teaspoon dried minced onion**
- **1 teaspoon granulated garlic**
- **1 teaspoon sesame seeds**
- **1 teaspoon poppy seeds**
- **¼ teaspoon coarse salt**

1. Preheat air fryer to 350°F.
2. Spray bagel slices generously with nonstick cooking spray. Cook 7 to 8 minutes or until golden brown, shaking occasionally during cooking.
3. Meanwhile, combine cream cheese, green onion, minced onion, garlic, sesame seeds, poppy seeds and salt in medium bowl; mix well. Serve with bagel chips.

MAKES 2 CUPS DIP

SWEET AND SPICY WINGS

2 pounds chicken wings, tips removed
1 tablespoon olive oil
1 teaspoon garlic powder
½ teaspoon salt
½ teaspoon onion powder
½ teaspoon paprika
¼ cup hot pepper sauce
2 tablespoons honey
2 tablespoons chili garlic sauce
Lemon wedges and favorite dipping sauces (optional)

1. Pat wings dry with paper towels; place in medium bowl. Drizzle with oil; sprinkle with garlic powder, salt, onion powder and paprika and toss to coat.
2. Preheat air fryer to 400°F. Spray basket with nonstick cooking spray.
3. Cook wings in single layer 20 to 25 minutes or until golden brown and crisp, turning halfway through cooking.
4. Meanwhile, combine hot pepper sauce, honey and chili garlic sauce in large bowl; mix well.
5. Add hot cooked wings to bowl with sauce; toss to coat. Serve with lemon wedges and dipping sauces, if desired.

MAKES 4 SERVINGS

TIP: To make the wings slightly less sticky and easier to eat, return them to the air fryer after coating them with sauce and cook for 3 minutes.

CRUNCHY AIR-FRIED GNOCCHI

- **1 package (about 17 ounces) shelf-stable gnocchi**
- **3 tablespoons grated Parmesan cheese**
- **1 teaspoon Italian seasoning**
- **¾ teaspoon garlic powder**
- **½ teaspoon salt**
- **¼ teaspoon black pepper**
- **2 tablespoons olive oil**
- **Pizza or marinara sauce (optional)**

1. Preheat air fryer to 400°F.
2. Place gnocchi in large bowl. Sprinkle with cheese, Italian seasoning, garlic powder, salt and pepper; drizzle with oil and toss to coat.
3. Cook gnocchi about 10 minutes or until lightly browned and crisp, shaking halfway through cooking. Serve warm with pizza sauce, if desired.

MAKES 4 TO 6 SERVINGS

BLISTERED SHISHITO PEPPERS

- 1 package (8 ounces) shishito peppers
- 1 teaspoon olive oil
- 1 tablespoon lemon juice
- ¼ teaspoon sea salt

1. Preheat air fryer to 400°F.
2. Combine peppers and oil in medium bowl; toss to coat.
3. Cook peppers 5 to 7 minutes or until blistered and browned in spots, shaking several times during cooking.
4. Return peppers to medium bowl. Drizzle with lemon juice and sprinkle with salt; toss to coat.

MAKES 4 SERVINGS

VARIATION: For Asian-flavored peppers, substitute dark sesame oil for the olive oil and soy sauce for the lemon juice. Cook as directed above.

PITA CHEESE STRAWS

- 3 pita bread rounds
- 2 tablespoons butter, melted
- 1 clove garlic, minced
- 1 teaspoon Italian seasoning
- ¾ teaspoon salt
- ¼ cup grated Parmesan cheese
- French onion dip (optional)

1 Split pita rounds in half horizontally; separate each into two rounds. Combine butter, garlic and Italian seasoning in small bowl; mix well.

2 Preheat air fryer to 330°F. Brush tops of pitas with butter mixture; sprinkle with salt and cheese. Cut into ½-inch strips with pizza cutter.

3 Cook pita strips in single layer 6 to 8 minutes or until edges are golden brown. Serve with dip, if desired.

MAKES 6 SERVINGS

MINI CHICKPEA CAKES

- 1 can (about 15 ounces) chickpeas, rinsed and drained
- 1 cup grated carrots
- ⅓ cup seasoned dry bread crumbs
- ¼ cup creamy Italian salad dressing, plus additional for dipping
- 1 egg

1. Coarsely mash chickpeas in medium bowl with fork or potato masher. Stir in carrots, bread crumbs, ¼ cup dressing and egg; mix well.
2. Shape chickpea mixture into 24 patties, using about 1 tablespoon mixture for each.
3. Preheat air fryer to 370°F. Spray basket with nonstick cooking spray.
4. Cook patties in single layer 10 minutes or until browned, turning halfway through cooking. Serve warm with additional dressing, if desired.

MAKES 2 DOZEN CAKES

JELLY-FILLED DOUGHNUT BITES

- **1 container (about 7 ounces) refrigerated biscuits (10 biscuits)**
- **¼ cup coarse sugar**
- **1 cup strawberry preserves***

If preserves are very chunky, purée in food processor 10 seconds or press through fine-mesh sieve.

1. Separate biscuits. Cut each biscuit in half; roll dough into balls to create 20 balls.
2. Preheat air fryer to 370°F. Place sugar in large bowl. Spray dough balls with nonstick cooking spray.
3. Cook doughnuts in batches 5 to 6 minutes or until golden brown, shaking occasionally and spraying again with cooking spray. Roll warm doughnuts in sugar to coat.
4. Fit piping bag with medium round tip; fill bag with preserves. Poke hole in side of each doughnut with paring knife; fill with preserves. Serve immediately.

MAKES 20 DOUGHNUTS

PARMESAN PICKLE CHIPS

4 large whole dill pickles

½ cup all-purpose flour

½ teaspoon salt

2 eggs

½ cup panko bread crumbs

2 tablespoons grated Parmesan cheese

Ranch dressing or garlic mayonnaise (optional)

1 Line baking sheet with paper towels. Cut pickles diagonally into ¼-inch slices; place on prepared baking sheet. Pat tops of pickles with paper towels to absorb excess moisture.

2 Combine flour and salt in shallow dish. Beat eggs in another shallow dish. Combine panko and cheese in third shallow dish.

3 Coat pickles with flour. Dip in eggs, letting excess drip back into dish, then roll in panko mixture to coat.

4 Preheat air fryer to 390°F. Cook pickles in batches 8 to 10 minutes or until golden brown. Serve with dressing, if desired.

MAKES 8 SERVINGS

CHEESY PROTEIN SNACKS

- 1 cup self-rising flour
- 1 cup cottage cheese
- ½ cup (2 ounces) shredded Cheddar cheese
- Pinch black pepper

1. Combine flour, cottage cheese, Cheddar and pepper in medium bowl; stir until rough dough forms.
2. Turn out dough onto lightly floured surface; knead several times until dough is smooth.
3. Preheat air fryer to 330°F. Cut two 8-inch squares of parchment paper.
4. Divide dough in half. Pat or roll each half into 6-inch square; place on parchment squares. Cut into 1-inch squares; separate squares slightly.
5. Cook dough on parchment 3 minutes or until firm and lightly browned. Serve warm or cool completely.

MAKES 4 SERVINGS

Poultry

AIR FRYER ROASTED CHICKEN

- 1 teaspoon salt
- ½ teaspoon garlic powder
- ½ teaspoon paprika
- ¼ teaspoon dried thyme
- ¼ teaspoon black pepper
- 1 whole chicken (3½ to 4 pounds)
- 1 tablespoon olive oil

1. Preheat air fryer to 350°F.
2. Combine salt, garlic powder, paprika, thyme and pepper in small bowl; mix well.
3. Pat chicken dry with paper towels. Tuck wing tips under. Brush oil all over chicken. Sprinkle half of seasoning mixture over breast side of chicken.
4. Place chicken breast side down in air fryer basket; sprinkle with remaining seasoning mixture.
5. Cook chicken 35 minutes. Turn chicken with tongs; cook 20 to 25 minutes or until cooked through (165°F). Remove to cutting board; tent with foil and let stand 10 minutes before carving.

MAKES 4 SERVINGS

PARMESAN CHICKEN TENDERS

- **1 cup plain yogurt**
- **1 pound chicken tenders**
- **⅓ cup yellow cornmeal**
- **⅓ cup plain dry bread crumbs**
- **¼ cup shredded Parmesan cheese**
- **2 tablespoons all-purpose flour**
- **1 teaspoon garlic powder**
- **½ teaspoon paprika**
- **¼ teaspoon salt**
- **Garlic mayonnaise, ketchup or favorite dipping sauce**

1. Place yogurt in medium bowl. Add chicken; stir to coat. Combine cornmeal, bread crumbs, cheese, flour, garlic powder, paprika and salt in shallow dish; mix well.
2. Preheat air fryer to 380°F. Spray basket with nonstick cooking spray.
3. Dip chicken tenders, one at a time, in cornmeal mixture; turn to coat.
4. Cook chicken in single layer* 10 to 12 minutes or until golden brown and no longer pink in center, turning halfway through cooking. Serve with garlic mayonnaise.

**Make sure there is space between tenders or chicken will not be crisp.*

MAKES 4 SERVINGS

CHICKEN FAJITA QUESADILLAS

- **8 ounces boneless skinless chicken breasts, cut into thin strips (about ¼ inch)**
- **2 teaspoons vegetable oil, divided**
- **½ teaspoon salt, divided**
- **2 medium onions, cut into ¼-inch slices**
- **1 red bell pepper, cut into ¼-inch slices**
- **⅔ cup salsa, plus additional for serving**
- **⅔ cup canned black beans, rinsed and drained**
- **8 (6-inch) flour tortillas**
- **2 cups (8 ounces) shredded Cheddar cheese**

1. Preheat air fryer to 380°F. Spray basket with nonstick cooking spray.
2. Place chicken in medium bowl. Drizzle with 1 teaspoon oil and sprinkle with ¼ teaspoon salt; toss to coat. Add to air fryer in single layer; cook 2 minutes.
3. Combine onions, bell pepper, remaining 1 teaspoon oil and ¼ teaspoon salt in same bowl; toss to coat. Add vegetables to air fryer; shake to combine with chicken. Cook about 8 minutes or edges of chicken and vegetables are beginning to brown, shaking every few minutes. Remove to clean bowl; add ⅔ cup salsa and beans and stir to blend. Wipe out air fryer basket with paper towel. *Reduce temperature of air fryer to 350°F.*
4. Place tortillas on work surface. Sprinkle half of each tortilla with 2 tablespoons cheese; top with ½ cup chicken mixture and remaining cheese. Fold tortillas in half over filling.
5. Spray basket with nonstick cooking spray. Place quesadillas in single layer in basket; spray with cooking spray. Place metal trivet, metal measuring cup or dinner knife on top of quesadillas to prevent tops of tortillas from opening.
6. Cook quesadillas 3 to 4 minutes or until cheese is melted and tortillas are lightly browned. Transfer to cutting board; cut into wedges. Serve with additional salsa, if desired.

MAKES 4 SERVINGS

TACO CHICKEN DRUMSTICKS

8 chicken drumsticks (3 to 3½ pounds)

1 package (1 ounce) taco seasoning mix

1 cup sour cream

1 cup taco sauce, divided

1. Preheat air fryer to 400°F. Sprinkle seasoning mix over chicken.
2. Cook chicken in single layer 20 minutes or until until cooked through (165°F), turning halfway through cooking.
3. Meanwhile, combine sour cream and ½ cup taco sauce* in small bowl; mix well.
4. Brush chicken with some of remaining taco sauce; cook 1 minute. Turn and brush with taco sauce; cook 1 minute or until chicken is lightly browned and crisp. Serve with sauce for dipping.

**For a chunkier dipping sauce, subsitute ½ cup chunky salsa for ½ cup taco sauce.*

MAKES 4 SERVINGS

BUFFALO CHICKEN WRAPS

2 boneless skinless chicken breasts (about 4 ounces each)

4 tablespoons buffalo wing sauce, divided

1 cup broccoli coleslaw mix

½ tablespoon blue cheese dressing

2 (8-inch) whole wheat tortillas, warmed

1. Place chicken in large resealable food storage bag. Add 2 tablespoons buffalo sauce; seal bag and turn to coat. Marinate in refrigerator 15 minutes.
2. Preheat air fryer to 370°F. Cook chicken 14 to 19 minutes or until no longer pink in center. Set aside to cool 5 minutes.
3. Cut chicken into thin slices; place in medium bowl. Add remaining 2 tablespoons buffalo sauce; stir to coat.
4. Combine coleslaw mix and blue cheese dressing in small bowl; mix well. Spoon chicken and coleslaw down center of tortillas; roll up to enclose filling. Cut in half diagonally.

MAKES 2 SERVINGS

TIP: If you don't like the spicy flavor of buffalo wing sauce, substitute your favorite barbecue sauce.

EASY TURKEY TURNOVERS

1 package (about 8 ounces) refrigerated crescent roll sheet

2 tablespoons honey mustard, plus additional for serving

3 ounces thinly sliced deli turkey

¾ cup broccoli coleslaw mix

1 egg, beaten

1 Unroll dough on lightly floured surface. Use cookie cutter, biscuit cutter or drinking glass to cut out six 3½-inch circles.

2 Brush 2 tablespoons mustard lightly over dough; top with turkey and coleslaw mix. Brush edges of dough with egg. Fold dough circles in half over filling; press edges with tines of fork to seal. Brush tops of turnovers with egg.

3 Preheat air fryer to 370°F. Spray basket with nonstick cooking spray.

4 Cook turnovers in batches 6 to 7 minutes or until golden brown. Let stand 5 minutes before serving. Serve warm or at room temperature with additional honey mustard, if desired.

MAKES 6 SERVINGS

BANG BANG CHICKEN

- ½ cup mayonnaise
- ¼ cup sweet chili sauce
- 1½ teaspoons hot pepper sauce
- ½ cup all-purpose flour
- ¾ cup panko bread crumbs
- 1 pound boneless skinless chicken breasts, cut into 1-inch pieces
- Hot cooked rice (optional)
- 2 green onions, chopped

1. Combine mayonnaise, chili sauce and hot pepper sauce in medium bowl; mix well. Reserve half of sauce for serving; pour remaining half into shallow dish.
2. Place flour in separate shallow dish. Place panko in third shallow dish. Coat chicken with flour. Dip in sauce mixture; turn to coat. Roll in panko to coat completely. Spray chicken with nonstick cooking spray.
3. Preheat air fryer to 390°F. Line basket with parchment paper.
4. Cook chicken in single layer 10 to 12 minutes or until golden brown and cooked through. Serve over rice, if desired. Drizzle with reserved sauce; sprinkle with green onions.

MAKES 4 SERVINGS

GARLIC CHICKEN WITH ROASTED VEGETABLES

- **3 tablespoons olive oil, divided**
- **2 cloves garlic, minced**
- **1¾ teaspoons salt, divided**
- **1 teaspoon dried oregano**
- **1 teaspoon paprika**
- **¾ teaspoon black pepper, divided**
- **4 boneless skinless chicken breasts (4 to 6 ounces each)**
- **2 cups Brussels sprouts, trimmed and halved**
- **2 small onions, cut into wedges**
- **1 cup frozen crinkle-cut carrots**

1. Combine 2 tablespoons oil, garlic, 1 teaspoon salt, oregano, paprika and ½ teaspoon pepper in small bowl; mix well. Brush over chicken.
2. Preheat air fryer to 370°F. Line basket with parchment paper.
3. Cook chicken in single layer 15 to 20 minutes or until chicken is browned and no longer pink in center. Remove to plate; tent with foil to keep warm. *Increase air fryer temperature to 390°F.*
4. Combine Brussels sprouts, onions, carrots and remaining 1 tablespoon oil in medium bowl; toss to coat. Season with remaining ¾ teaspoon salt and ¼ teaspoon pepper.
5. Cook vegetables in batches 6 to 8 minutes or until tender and lightly browned, shaking halfway through cooking.

MAKES 4 SERVINGS

ZESTY ITALIAN CHICKEN NUGGETS

- **2 boneless skinless chicken breasts (4 to 6 ounces each)**
- **¼ cup zesty Italian salad dressing**
- **2 tablespoons honey**
- **¾ teaspoon salt**
- **¼ teaspoon black pepper**

1 Cut chicken into 1-inch pieces; place in large resealable food storage bag.

2 Whisk dressing, honey, salt and pepper in medium bowl until well blended. Pour over chicken; seal bag and turn to coat. Marinate in refrigerator 30 minutes to 1 hour.

3 Preheat air fryer to 370°F. Line basket with parchment paper. Remove chicken from marinade; discard marinade.

4 Cook chicken in batches 10 to 12 minutes or until cooked through, shaking halfway through cooking.

MAKES 4 SERVINGS

CHICKEN CHEDDAR BURGERS

1¼ pounds ground chicken or turkey
1 cup plain dry bread crumbs
½ cup finely chopped red bell pepper
½ cup ground walnuts
¼ cup sliced green onions
¼ cup light beer
2 tablespoons chopped fresh parsley
2 tablespoons lemon juice
2 cloves garlic, minced
1 teaspoon salt
¼ teaspoon black pepper
4 slices white Cheddar cheese
4 whole wheat buns
Dijon mustard and lettuce leaves

1 Combine chicken, bread crumbs, bell pepper, walnuts, green onions, beer, parsley, lemon juice, garlic, salt and black pepper in large bowl; mix gently. Shape into four patties.

2 Preheat air fryer to 390°F. Spray basket with nonstick cooking spray.

3 Cook patties 12 to 14 minutes or until cooked through (165°F), turning halfway through cooking. Place cheese on patties; cook 1 minute or just until cheese begins to melt.

4 Serve burgers on buns with mustard and lettuce.

MAKES 4 SERVINGS

CRISPY CRUNCHY CHICKEN BITES

1 pound boneless skinless chicken breasts

½ cup ranch dressing, plus additional for serving

2 cups panko bread crumbs

1. Cut chicken into 1-inch pieces. Place ½ cup dressing in shallow dish. Spread panko in another shallow dish.
2. Dip chicken into dressing; shake off excess. Roll in panko to coat. Spray chicken with nonstick cooking spray.
3. Preheat air fryer to 370°F. Line basket with parchment paper.
4. Cook chicken in batches 8 to 10 minutes or until chicken is golden brown and cooked through. Serve with additional ranch dressing.

MAKES 6 SERVINGS

BALSAMIC CHICKEN

- **2 cloves garlic, minced**
- **1½ teaspoons minced fresh rosemary *or* ½ teaspoon dried rosemary**
- **¾ teaspoon black pepper**
- **½ teaspoon salt**
- **6 boneless skinless chicken breasts (4 to 6 ounces each)**
- **1 tablespoon olive oil**
- **¼ cup balsamic vinegar**

1. Combine garlic, rosemary, pepper and salt in small bowl; mix well. Place chicken in large bowl; drizzle with oil and rub with spice mixture. Cover and refrigerate several hours.
2. Preheat air fryer to 390°F. Spray basket with nonstick cooking spray.
3. Cook chicken in single layer 15 to 20 minutes or until no longer pink in center. Drizzle with vinegar.

MAKES 6 SERVINGS

TASTY TURKEY QUESADILLAS

- 8 (8-inch) flour tortillas
- 1 cup finely chopped cooked turkey or chicken
- ½ cup salsa, plus additional for serving
- 1 cup (4 ounces) shredded Cheddar cheese
- 2 tablespoons chopped fresh cilantro
- 1 tablespoon olive oil
- Sour cream (optional)

1. Place four tortillas on work surface; top evenly with turkey, ½ cup salsa, cheese and cilantro. Top with remaining four tortillas.

2. Preheat air fryer to 350°F. Spray basket with nonstick cooking spray.

3. Place one quesadilla in basket; spray with cooking spray. Place metal trivet, measuring cup or dinner knife on top of quesadilla to prevent top tortilla from blowing off.

4. Cook 4 minutes; turn and cook 2 to 3 minutes or until lightly browned. Repeat with remaining quesadillas. Cut into wedges; serve with additional salsa and sour cream, if desired.

MAKES 4 SERVINGS

ASIAN BARBECUE SKEWERS

- ½ **cup reduce-sodium soy sauce**
- ⅓ **cup packed brown sugar**
- 2 **tablespoons sesame oil**
- 2 **teaspoons garlic powder**
- ⅛ **teaspoon red pepper flakes (optional)**
- 2 **pounds boneless skinless chicken thighs, cut into 1-inch-wide strips**
- 1 **tablespoon barbecue sauce**
- 1 **tablespoon toasted sesame seeds (optional)**

1 Combine soy sauce, brown sugar, oil, garlic powder and red pepper flakes, if desired, in medium bowl; mix well. Remove ⅓ cup mixture to small bowl; set aside.

2 Add chicken to remaining mixture; stir to coat. Cover and marinate at room temperature 30 minutes or up to 8 hours in refrigerator. Soak 16 (7-inch) wooden skewers in water 20 minutes to prevent burning.

3 Thread chicken onto skewers. Preheat air fryer to 370°F. Line basket with parchment paper.

4 Cook skewers in single layer 12 minutes or until chicken is cooked through, turning halfway through cooking.

5 Stir barbecue sauce into reserved soy sauce mixture; brush over skewers immediately after cooking. Sprinkle with sesame seeds, if desired.

MAKES 4 TO 6 SERVINGS

LEMON CHICKEN

- 1 egg yolk
- 2 teaspoons soy sauce
- 1½ cups panko bread crumbs
- ⅛ teaspoon salt
- ⅛ teaspoon black pepper
- 1 pound chicken tenders or 1 pound boneless skinless chicken breasts, cut into 1-inch strips
- 1 cup chicken broth
- 1 tablespoon cornstarch
- 1 teaspoon vegetable oil
- 1 clove garlic, minced
- Grated peel of 1 lemon
- 1 teaspoon sugar
- 1½ to 2½ teaspoons lemon juice

1. Beat egg yolk and soy sauce in shallow dish. Combine panko, salt and pepper in another shallow dish. Dip chicken strips in egg mixture, then roll in panko to coat. Spray both sides of chicken with nonstick cooking spray.
2. Preheat air fryer to 400°F. Line basket with parchment paper. Place chicken in single layer in basket; spray with nonstick cooking spray.
3. Cook chicken 10 to 12 minutes or until golden brown and cooked through, turning halfway through cooking. (Make sure there is space between tenders or chicken will not be crisp.)
4. Meanwhile, stir broth into cornstarch in small bowl until smooth. Heat oil in small saucepan over low heat. Add garlic; cook and stir 1 minute or until softened. Stir in lemon peel. Add broth mixture and sugar; cook and stir over medium heat 2 minutes or until thickened. Stir in 1½ teaspoons lemon juice; taste and add additional lemon juice, if desired. Drizzle sauce over chicken.

MAKES 4 SERVINGS

TIP: To add a little spice to the chicken, stir ⅛ teaspoon ground red pepper into the panko mixture.

RANCH ROASTED CHICKEN AND CORN

- **4 chicken drumsticks**
- **2 ears corn on the cob, husks and silk removed**
- **1 tablespoons butter, melted**
- **2 tablespoons ranch dressing mix (about half of 1-ounce package)**

1. Preheat air fryer to 380°F. Spray basket with nonstick cooking spray.
2. Brush chicken and corn with butter; sprinkle with seasoning mix, turning to coat all sides.
3. Cook chicken in single layer 5 minutes. Add corn to basket next to chicken; cook 5 minutes.
4. Turn chicken; cook 5 minutes. Turn corn; cook 5 minutes or until corn is tender and chicken is cooked through (165°F).

MAKES 2 SERVINGS

SAVORY PARMESAN-CRUSTED CHICKEN

- **4 boneless skinless chicken breasts (4 to 6 ounces each)**
- **½ cup panko bread crumbs**
- **¼ cup grated Parmesan cheese**
- **1 package (about 1 ounce) ranch dressing mix**
- **½ teaspoon black pepper**
- **2 tablespoons ranch or Caesar dressing***

****Or substitute plain yogurt or mayonnaise for the dressing.***

1. If chicken pieces are not even, place chicken between sheets of plastic wrap and pound to ½-inch thickness with meat mallet or rolling pin.
2. Preheat air fryer to 370°F. Spray basket with nonstick cooking spray.
3. Combine panko, cheese, ranch dressing mix and pepper in shallow dish. Brush chicken with dressing; roll in panko mixture to coat.
4. Cook chicken in single layer 12 to 15 minutes or until golden brown and no longer pink in center, turning carefully after 8 minutes.

MAKES 4 SERVINGS

CHICKEN TENDERS WITH BLUE CHEESE DIPPING SAUCE

1 egg

⅔ cup bran cereal flake crumbs* (about 1⅓ cups bran flakes)

1 pound chicken tenders (8 tenders)

¼ cup buttermilk

¼ cup sour cream

3 tablespoons crumbled blue cheese

2 teaspoons minced green onion

¼ teaspoon salt

⅛ teaspoon black pepper

To make cereal crumbs, pulse cereal in a food processor or crush in a resealable food storage bag with a rolling pin.

1 Beat egg in shallow dish. Spread cereal crumbs in another shallow dish.

2 Dip chicken in egg, letting excess drip back into dish. Roll in cereal crumbs to coat. Spray both sides with nonstick cooking spray.

3 Preheat air fryer to 380°F.

4 Cook chicken in single layer* about 14 minutes or until golden brown and no longer pink in center, turning halfway through cooking.

5 Meanwhile, whisk buttermilk, sour cream, cheese, green onion, salt and pepper in medium bowl until well blended. Serve with chicken.

**Make sure there is space between tenders or chicken will not be crisp.*

MAKES 4 SERVINGS

QUICK CHICKEN FLAUTAS

2 cups shredded cooked chicken*

⅔ cup chunky salsa

8 (6-inch) flour tortillas

Sour cream and guacamole (optional)

****Use a supermarket rotisserie chicken for convenience; one chicken will yield about 4 cups shredded meat.***

1 Combine chicken and salsa in medium bowl; mix well. Place one tortilla on work surface; spread heaping ¼ cup chicken mixture on bottom half of tortilla. Roll up tightly into cylinder; secure with toothpick. Repeat with remaining tortillas and filling.

2 Preheat air fryer to 360°F. Spray basket with nonstick cooking spray. Place half of tortilla rolls in basket, seam side down; spray with cooking spray.

3 Cook tortilla rolls 4 minutes; spray with cooking spray. Cook 2 to 3 minutes or until lightly browned. Repeat with remaining tortilla rolls.

4 Remove toothpicks; serve immediately with sour cream and guacamole, if desired.

MAKES 4 SERVINGS

HOT SWEET MUSTARD CHICKEN

4 cups small pretzel twists

8 boneless skinless chicken thighs* (about 2 pounds)

½ teaspoon salt

¼ teaspoon black pepper

½ cup hot sweet mustard

****Boneless skinless chicken breasts can also be used; reduce cooking time to 12 to 15 minutes.***

1 Place pretzels in large resealable food storage bag; seal bag and crush pretzels with rolling pin, meat mallet or heavy skillet. (Pretzels should yield about 2 cups crumbs.) Place pretzel crumbs in shallow dish.

2 Season chicken with salt and pepper. Generously brush all sides of chicken with mustard. Roll chicken in pretzel crumbs to coat, gently pressing crumbs into mustard to adhere.

3 Preheat air fryer to 380°F. Line basket with parchment paper. Arrange chicken in single layer in basket; spray with nonstick cooking spray.

4 Cook chicken 8 minutes; turn and spray with cooking spray. Cook 8 to 10 minutes or until chicken is cooked through.

MAKES 4 TO 6 SERVINGS

PESTO TURKEY BURGERS

- **1 pound ground turkey**
- **2 tablespoons grated onion**
- **2 tablespoons pesto sauce, divided**
- **2 tablespoons chopped sun-dried tomatoes, divided**
- **¼ teaspoon salt**
- **¼ teaspoon black pepper**
- **¼ cup mayonnaise**
- **4 hamburger buns, split**
- **Lettuce leaves, tomato slices and red onion slices**

1. Preheat air fryer to 380°F.
2. Combine turkey, onion, 1 tablespoon pesto sauce, 1 tablespoon sun-dried tomato, salt and pepper in medium bowl; mix gently. Shape mixture into four patties about ½ inch thick.
3. Cook patties 7 minutes; turn and cook 3 to 5 minutes or until browned and cooked through (165°).
4. Meanwhile, combine mayonnaise, remaining 1 tablespoon pesto sauce and 1 tablespoon sun-dried tomato in small bowl; mix well.
5. Serve burgers on buns with lettuce, tomato, onion and mayonnaise mixture.

MAKES 4 SERVINGS

LEMON PEPPER CHICKEN

⅓ cup lemon juice

¼ cup finely chopped onion

2 tablespoons olive oil

1 tablespoon packed brown sugar

1 tablespoon black pepper

3 cloves garlic, minced

2 teaspoons grated lemon peel

½ teaspoon salt

4 boneless skinless chicken breasts (4 to 6 ounces each)

1. Combine lemon juice, onion, oil, brown sugar, pepper, garlic, lemon peel and salt in small bowl; mix well.

2. Place chicken in large resealable food storage bag. Pour marinade over chicken; seal bag and turn to coat. Refrigerate at least 4 hours or overnight.

3. Preheat air fryer to 370°F. Line basket with parchment paper or foil; spray with nonstick cooking spray.

4. Remove chicken from marinade; discard marinade. Cook chicken in single layer 15 to 20 minutes or until browned and no longer pink in center.

MAKES 4 SERVINGS

BUTTERMILK CHICKEN FINGERS

- **1½ cups biscuit baking mix**
- **1 cup buttermilk***
- **1 egg**
- **12 chicken tenders (about 1½ pounds), patted dry**
- **⅓ cup mayonnaise**
- **1 tablespoon honey**
- **1 tablespoon Dijon mustard**
- **1 tablespoon packed dark brown sugar**

Or substitute 1 tablespoon vinegar or lemon juice plus enough milk to equal 1 cup. Stir; let stand 5 minutes.

1. Place biscuit mix in shallow dish. Beat buttermilk and egg in another shallow dish.
2. Roll chicken tenders, one at a time, in biscuit mix to coat. Dip in buttermilk mixture; roll again in biscuit mix.
3. Preheat air fryer to 390°F. Cook chicken in single layer* 10 to 12 minutes or until golden brown and no longer pink in center, turning halfway through cooking.
4. Meanwhile, combine mayonnaise, honey, mustard and brown sugar in small bowl; mix well. Serve with chicken.

**Make sure there is space between tenders or chicken will not be crisp.*

MAKES 4 SERVINGS

EASY ASIAN CHICKEN

- **¼ cup soy sauce**
- **2 tablespoons lemon juice**
- **1½ teaspoons honey**
- **1 teaspoon minced garlic**
- **1 teaspoon dark sesame oil**
- **½ teaspoon dry mustard**
- **½ teaspoon grated fresh ginger *or* ¼ teaspoon ground ginger**
- **⅛ teaspoon red pepper flakes**
- **4 boneless skinless chicken breasts (about 6 ounces each)**

1. Combine soy sauce, juice, honey, garlic, oil, mustard, ginger and red pepper flakes in small bowl; mix well.
2. Place chicken in large resealable food storage bag. Pour soy sauce mixture over chicken; seal bag and turn to coat. Marinate in refrigerator 1 hour or overnight.
3. Preheat air fryer to 360°F. Remove chicken from marinade; discard marinade.
4. Cook chicken in single layer 16 to 20 minutes or until no longer pink in center, turning halfway through cooking. Let stand 5 minutes before slicing.

MAKES 4 SERVINGS

CRISPY RANCH CHICKEN

- **1 cup cornflake crumbs**
- **1 teaspoon salt**
- **1 teaspoon dried rosemary**
- **½ teaspoon black pepper**
- **1 cup ranch salad dressing**
- **2 pounds bone-in chicken thighs and drumsticks**

1. Combine cornflake crumbs, salt, rosemary and pepper in shallow dish. Pour dressing into another shallow dish.
2. Dip chicken in dressing; turn to coat. Roll chicken in crumb mixture to coat.
3. Preheat air fryer to 370°F. Spray basket with nonstick cooking spray. Place chicken in single layer in basket; spray with cooking spray.
4. Cook chicken 20 to 25 minutes or until cooked through (165°F).

MAKES 4 SERVINGS

VARIATION: To add an Italian flavor to this dish, substitute 1¼ cups Italian-seasoned dry bread crumbs and ¼ cup grated Parmesan cheese for the cornflake crumbs, rosemary, salt and pepper. Prepare recipe as directed.

ALL-AMERICAN BURGERS

- **1 pound ground beef**
- **2 teaspoons Worcestershire sauce**
- **1 teaspoon onion powder**
- **¾ teaspoon garlic powder**
- **½ teaspoon salt**
- **½ teaspoon black pepper**
- **4 thick slices American or Cheddar cheese**
- **4 slices bacon, crisp-cooked and crumbled *or* 4 tablespoons bacon bits (optional)**
- **4 hamburger buns, split**
- **Lettuce leaves**

1. Combine beef, Worcestershire sauce, onion powder, garlic powder, salt and pepper in medium bowl; mix gently.
2. Shape mixture into four patties about ½ inch thick. Press small indentation into center of each patty with thumb or fingertips.
3. Preheat air fryer to 360°F.
4. Cook patties in single layer 6 minutes; turn and cook 2 to 3 minutes or cooked through (160°F).
5. Top each burger with cheese slice; cook 30 seconds to 1 minute or until cheese begins to melt. Sprinkle with bacon, if desired. Serve burgers on buns with lettuce.

MAKES 4 SERVINGS

SIMPLE SALSA STEAK

- **1½ cups medium salsa**
- **3 tablespoons lime juice**
- **1½ tablespoons olive oil**
- **¾ teaspoon chipotle chili powder**
- **¾ teaspoon ground cumin**
- **1½ pounds flank steak**
- **1 green onion, finely chopped**

1. Combine salsa, lime juice, oil, chili powder and cumin in medium bowl; mix well. Reserve half of mixture in small bowl for serving; set aside.
2. Place steak in large resealable food storage bag. Pour remaining salsa mixture over steak; seal bag and turn to coat, massaging marinade into steak. Marinate in refrigerator at least 2 hours or overnight.
3. Preheat air fryer to 400°F. Spray basket with nonstick cooking spray.
4. Remove steak from marinade; discard marinade. Brush off any large pieces of marinade from steak.
5. Cook steak 5 minutes;* turn and cook 5 minutes for medium rare (130° to 135°F) or until desired doneness. Remove to cutting board; tent with foil and let stand 10 minutes.
6. Cut steak into thin slices against the grain. Stir green onion into reserved salsa mixture; serve with steak.

**If your air fryer basket cannot fit entire steak in single layer, cut steak in half and cook in two batches.*

MAKES 4 SERVINGS

PORK CHOPS WITH SPICY ORANGE CRANBERRY SAUCE

1 teaspoon chili powder
½ teaspoon salt
½ teaspoon ground cumin
¼ teaspoon ground allspice
¼ teaspoon black pepper
4 boneless pork chops (about 4 ounces each, 1 inch thick)
1 tablespoon canola oil
1 cup whole berry cranberry sauce
½ teaspoon grated orange peel
¼ teaspoon ground cinnamon
⅛ teaspoon red pepper flakes

1. Combine chili powder, salt, cumin, allspice and black pepper in small bowl; mix well. Pat pork chops dry with paper towel. Drizzle with oil; sprinkle both sides of pork with spice mixture.
2. Preheat air fryer to 380°F. Spray basket with nonstick cooking spray.
3. Cook pork chops in single layer 5 minutes; turn and cook 4 minutes or until pork is barely pink in center.
4. Meanwhile, combine cranberry sauce, orange peel, cinnamon and red pepper flakes in small bowl; mix well. Serve sauce with pork chops.

MAKES 4 SERVINGS

AIR-FRIED BEEF TAQUITOS

12 ounces ground beef

¼ cup chopped onion

1 tablespoon taco seasoning mix

6 corn tortillas

6 tablespoons shredded Cheddar cheese, plus additional for topping

Salsa, sour cream and guacamole (optional)

1 Cook beef and onion in large skillet over medium-high heat 6 to 8 minutes or until browned, stirring to break up meat. Drain fat. Add taco seasoning mix; cook and stir 2 minutes.

2 Spoon about 2 tablespoons beef mixture down center of each tortilla; top with 1 tablespoon cheese. Roll up tortillas to enclose filling; secure with toothpicks. Spray with nonstick cooking spray.

3 Preheat air fryer to 370°F.

4 Cook taquitos in single layer 3 to 4 minutes or until tortillas are browned and crisp.

5 Remove toothpicks before serving. Top with salsa, sour cream, guacamole and additional cheese, if desired.

MAKES 6 SERVINGS

VARIATION: Substitute ground turkey, chicken or pork for the ground beef in the taquito filling, or use leftover chopped cooked meat.

OPEN-FACED STEAK AND BLUE CHEESE SANDWICHES

- **4 boneless beef top loin (strip) or tenderloin steaks (¾ inch thick)**
- **2 teaspoons olive oil**
- **¾ teaspoon salt**
- **¼ teaspoon black pepper**
- **8 thin slices blue cheese**
- **4 slices ciabatta bread, toasted**

1. Bring steaks to room temperature. Rub steaks with oil; season with salt and pepper.
2. Preheat air fryer to 400°F.
3. Cook steaks 5 minutes; turn and cook 4 minutes for medium rare (130° to 135°F) or until desired doneness. Remove to cutting board; tent with foil and let stand 5 minutes.
4. Cut steak into thin slices; season with additional salt. Place two slices cheese on each toast slice; top with steak. Serve immediately.

MAKES 4 SERVINGS

TIP: While steak is resting, cook thick slices of sweet onion in the air fryer. Brush with oil; sprinkle with salt and cook about 10 minutes or until softened and beginning to brown, turning halfway through cooking. Separate onions into rings after cooking.

ROASTED SAUSAGE WITH WHITE BEANS

- 2 tablespoons olive oil
- 10 fresh sage leaves (about 1 sprig)
- 2 cloves garlic, minced
- 1 can (about 14 ounces) diced tomatoes
- 2 cans (about 15 ounces each) cannellini beans, rinsed and drained
- ¼ teaspoon salt
- ⅛ teaspoon black pepper
- 1 pound uncooked mild or hot Italian sausage (4 links)

1. Heat oil in large skillet over medium-low heat. Add sage and garlic; cook 2 to 3 minutes or just until garlic begins to turn golden. Add tomatoes; bring to a simmer.
2. Stir in beans, salt and pepper; cook 15 minutes, stirring occasionally.
3. Meanwhile, preheat air fryer to 360°F.
4. Cook sausages in single layer 6 minutes; turn and cook about 6 minutes or until browned and cooked through. Serve sausages over beans.

MAKES 4 SERVINGS

STEAK AND MUSHROOM SUPPER

- **12 ounces boneless steak, cut into 1-inch pieces**
- **8 ounces sliced mushrooms**
- **1 onion, chopped**
- **3 tablespoons butter, melted, divided**
- **1 teaspoon Worcestershire sauce**
- **½ teaspoon garlic powder**
- **½ teaspoon salt**
- **¼ teaspoon black pepper**
- **Hot cooked egg noodles or rice (optional)**
- **Chopped fresh parsley (optional)**

1. Combine steak, mushrooms and onion in large bowl. Add 1½ tablespoons butter, Worcestershire sauce and garlic powder; toss to coat.
2. Preheat air fryer to 390°F. Line basket with foil.
3. Cook steak mixture 10 to 12 minutes or until steak is cooked to desired donenss, shaking occasionally during cooking.
4. Transfer to clean bowl. Drizzle with remaining 1½ tablespoons butter; sprinkle with salt and pepper and toss to coat. Serve over noodles and garnish with parsley, if desired.

MAKES 4 SERVINGS

PEPPERONI PIZZA BISCUITS

- **1 package (12 ounces) refrigerated flaky buttermilk biscuits (10 biscuits)**
- **1 package (5 ounces) mini pepperoni slices**
- **¼ cup chopped bell pepper (optional)**
- **2 teaspoons dried basil**
- **½ cup pizza sauce**
- **1½ cups (6 ounces) shredded mozzarella cheese**
- **Shredded Parmesan cheese (optional)**

1. Spray (2½-inch) silicone muffin cups with nonstick cooking spray.
2. Separate biscuits; split each biscuit in half horizontally to create 20 rounds. Place in prepared muffin cups.
3. Press 4 pepperoni slices into center of each round. Sprinkle with bell pepper, if desired, and basil. Spread pizza sauce over pepperoni; sprinkle with mozzarella.
4. Preheat air fryer to 370°F.
5. Cook in batches 14 to 16 minutes or until pizzas are golden brown. Sprinkle with Parmesan, if desired. Cool in muffin cups 2 minutes; remove to wire racks. Serve warm.

MAKES 20 MINI PIZZAS

KOREAN BEEF SALAD

- 2 tablespoons soy sauce
- 1 tablespoon cornstarch
- 1 tablespoon packed brown sugar
- 2 cloves garlic, minced
- 1 teaspoon toasted sesame seeds
- ½ teaspoon dark sesame oil
- ¼ teaspoon red pepper flakes
- 12 ounces boneless beef sirloin steak, cut into thin slices (about 1 inch wide and ¼ inch thick)
- Quick Asian Dressing (recipe follows)
- 12 ounces bok choy or Napa cabbage, cut into 1-inch pieces
- 1 small cucumber, quartered and thinly sliced
- 1 carrot, cut into julienne strips or shredded
- 1 cup snow peas, trimmed
- ½ cup fresh bean sprouts (optional)

1. Whisk soy sauce, cornstarch, brown sugar, garlic, sesame seeds, sesame oil and red pepper flakes in medium bowl until well blended. Add beef; stir to coat. Marinate at room temperature 30 minutes or refrigerate up to 24 hours.

2. Prepare Quick Asian Dressing. Combine bok choy, cucumber, carrot, snow peas and bean sprouts, if desired, in large bowl.

3. Preheat air fryer to 400°F. Spray basket with nonstick cooking spray.

4. Add beef in single layer; cook 5 to 7 minutes or until browned. Arrange beef over salad; serve with dressing.

MAKES 4 SERVINGS

QUICK ASIAN DRESSING: Whisk 3 tablespoons water, 3 tablespoons soy sauce, 2 tablespoons rice vinegar, 1½ tablespoons dark sesame oil, 1 tablespoon packed brown sugar and ¼ teaspoon red pepper flakes in small bowl until well blended.

JAMAICAN JERK PORK

- **2 green onions, minced**
- **2 tablespoons olive oil**
- **2 to 3 tablespoons jerk seasoning**
- **Grated peel and juice of 2 limes**
- **1½ tablespoons soy sauce**
- **2 cloves garlic, minced**
- **1½ teaspoons sugar**
- **¼ teaspoon salt**
- **4 thick bone-in pork chops (about 8 ounces each, 1½ to 2 inches thick)**

1. Combine green onions, oil, jerk seasoning, lime peel, lime juice, soy sauce, garlic, sugar and salt in medium bowl; mix well.
2. Place pork chops in large resealable food storage bag. Pour marinade over pork; seal bag and turn to coat. Refrigerate overnight, turning once or twice.
3. Preheat air fryer to 400°F. Spray basket with nonstick cooking spray. Remove pork from marinade; discard marinade.
4. Cook pork chops in single layer 7 minutes; turn and cook 7 minutes or until pork is 145°F. Let stand 5 minutes before serving.

MAKES 4 SERVINGS

CALIFORNIA BBQ BURGERS

- **4 tablespoons barbecue sauce, divided**
- **2 tablespoons mayonnaise**
- **1 medium onion, divided**
- **1 pound ground beef**
- **2 teaspoons olive oil**
- **½ teaspoon salt**
- **¼ teaspoon black pepper**
- **4 burger buns, split and toasted**
- **1 ripe avocado, sliced**

1. Combine 2 tablespoons barbecue sauce and mayonnaise in small bowl; set aside. Cut ½ inch off top of onion; finely chop. (You should have about 1½ tablespoons.) Cut remaining onion into ¼-inch-thick slices.

2. Combine beef, chopped onion and 1 tablespoon barbecue sauce in medium bowl; mix gently. Shape mixture into four patties (about ½ inch thick); press small indentation into center of each patty with thumb or fingertips.

3. Preheat air fryer to 360°F. Brush onion slices with oil. Cook 4 minutes or until softened and beginning to brown, shaking halfway through cooking time. Remove onion to small bowl; stir in remaining 1 tablespoon barbecue sauce.

4. Season both sides of patties with salt and pepper; place in single layer in air fryer basket. Cook 5 minutes; turn and cook 2 to 3 minutes or until cooked through (160°F).

5. Spread 1 tablespoon mayonnaise mixture on top half of each bun. Place burgers on bottom halves of buns; top with cooked onions, avocado and top halves of buns.

MAKES 4 SERVINGS

GNOCCHI WITH SAUSAGE, MUSHROOMS AND BUTTERNUT SQUASH

- **1 package (16 to 17 ounces) shelf-stable potato gnocchi**
- **1 package (12 ounces) cooked Italian-style pork or chicken sausages, cut into ¾-inch slices**
- **2½ cups cubed butternut squash (½-inch cubes, about 1 small squash)**
- **2 medium red onions, halved and cut into ¾-inch wedges**
- **8 ounces cremini and/or white mushrooms, cut into quarters**
- **3 tablespoons olive oil**
- **1½ teaspoons salt**
- **1 teaspoon garlic powder**
- **1 teaspoon Italian seasoning**
- **½ teaspoon black pepper**

1. Preheat air fryer to 400°F.
2. Combine gnocchi, sausage, squash, onions and mushrooms in large bowl.
3. Drizzle with oil; sprinkle with salt, garlic powder, Italian seasoning and black pepper and toss to coat. Add half of mixture to air fryer.
4. Cook 12 minutes or until vegetables are tender and gnocchi are lightly browned, shaking halfway through cooking. Remove to large bowl; cover to keep warm. Repeat with remaining half of gnocchi and vegetable mixture. Season with additional salt and pepper, if desired.

MAKES 4 TO 6 SERVINGS

GREEK-STYLE STEAK SANDWICHES

- **2 teaspoons Greek seasoning**
- **1 beef flank steak (about 1½ pounds)**
- **4 pita bread rounds, cut in half crosswise**
- **1 small cucumber, thinly sliced**
- **1 tomato, cut into thin wedges**
- **½ cup sliced red onion**
- **½ cup crumbled feta cheese**
- **¼ cup red wine vinaigrette**
- **1 cup plain yogurt**

1. Rub Greek seasoning over both sides of steak. Place on plate; cover and refrigerate 30 to 60 minutes.
2. Preheat air fryer to 400°F.
3. Cook steak 6 minutes; turn and cook about 6 minutes for medium rare (130° to 135°F) or until desired doneness. Remove to cutting board; tent with foil and let stand 10 minutes.
4. Slice steak into thin strips against the grain. Divide meat among pita halves; top with cucumber, tomato, onion and cheese. Drizzle with vinaigrette; serve with yogurt.

MAKES 4 SERVINGS

SOY GINGER SALMON

- ¼ cup reduced-sodium soy sauce
- 2 tablespoons packed brown sugar
- 1 tablespoon grated fresh ginger
- 1 tablespoon butter
- 1 teaspoon Dijon mustard
- 2 salmon fillets (about 6 ounces each, 1 to 1¼ inches thick)
- ⅛ teaspoon black pepper

1 Combine soy sauce, brown sugar and ginger in small saucepan; bring to a simmer over medium heat. Cook 5 minutes or until slightly reduced and thickened. Remove from heat. Add butter and mustard; stir until butter is melted and mixture is smooth.

2 Preheat air fryer to 390°F. Spray basket with nonstick cooking spray.

3 Season fish with pepper; brush with soy sauce mixture.

4 Cook fish 5 minutes; brush with soy sauce mixture. Cook 3 to 5 minutes or until fish begins to flake when tested with fork. Brush with remaining soy sauce mixture before serving.

MAKES 2 SERVINGS

ROASTED DILL SCROD WITH ASPARAGUS

- **1 teaspoon olive oil**
- **1 bunch (12 ounces) asparagus spears, trimmed**
- **1 tablespoon lemon juice**
- **4 scrod or cod fillets (4 to 6 ounces each)**
- **1 teaspoon dried dill weed**
- **½ teaspoon salt**
- **¼ teaspoon black pepper**
- **Paprika (optional)**

1. Preheat air fryer to 390°F. Line basket with parchment paper.
2. Drizzle oil over asparagus; roll spears to coat lightly with oil. Cook 8 to 10 minutes or until asparagus is tender. Remove to plate; tent with foil to keep warm.
3. Drizzle lemon juice over fish. Combine dill weed, salt and pepper in small bowl; sprinkle over fish.
4. Cook fish in single layer 10 to 12 minutes or until opaque in center and fish begins to flake when tested with fork. Sprinkle with paprika, if desired. Serve with asparagus.

MAKES 4 SERVINGS

BLACKENED CATFISH WITH SHORTCUT TARTAR SAUCE

Shortcut Tartar Sauce (recipe follows)
4 catfish fillets (4 to 6 ounces each)
2 teaspoons lemon juice
2 teaspoons blackened or Cajun seasoning blend
Hot cooked rice (optional)

1. Prepare Shortcut Tartar Sauce.
2. Preheat air fryer to 390°F. Pat fish dry with paper towel. Sprinkle with lemon juice; spray with nonstick cooking spray. Sprinkle with seasoning blend; spray again with cooking spray.
3. Cook fish in single layer 8 to 10 minutes or until fish begins to flake when tested with fork, turning halfway through cooking. Serve with tartar sauce and rice, if desired.

MAKES 4 SERVINGS

SHORTCUT TARTAR SAUCE

½ cup mayonnaise
¼ cup sweet pickle relish
2 teaspoons lemon juice

Combine mayonnaise, relish and lemon juice in small bowl; mix well. Cover and refrigerate until ready to serve.

MAKES ABOUT ¾ CUP

SPEEDY PARMESAN SALMON

¼ cup mayonnaise

3 tablespoons grated Parmesan cheese

¼ teaspoon garlic powder

⅛ teaspoon ground red pepper (optional)

4 salmon fillets (4 to 6 ounces each)

14 buttery round crackers, crushed (½ cup cracker crumbs)

1. Combine mayonnaise, cheese, garlic power and red pepper, if desired, in small bowl; mix well.
2. Pat fish dry with paper towel; spread mayonnaise mixture evenly over fish. Top with cracker crumbs, pressing in gently to adhere.
3. Preheat air fryer to 370°F. Spray basket with nonstick cooking spray.
4. Cook fish 8 to 10 minutes or until fish begins to flake when tested with fork.

MAKES 4 SERVINGS

COCONUT CURRY SHRIMP

- **½ cup shredded unsweetened coconut**
- **¾ teaspoon curry powder**
- **½ teaspoon salt**
- **1 pound large raw shrimp, peeled and deveined**
- **3 tablespoons butter, melted**
- **Prepared chutney (optional)**

1. Combine coconut, curry powder and salt in shallow dish. Combine shrimp and butter in medium bowl; stir to coat. Dip shrimp in coconut mixture, pressing lightly to adhere.
2. Preheat air fryer to 350°F. Spray basket with nonstick cooking spray.
3. Cook shrimp in batches 8 to 10 minutes or until shrimp are pink and opaque, turning halfway through cooking. Serve with chutney, if desired.

MAKES 4 SERVINGS

SALMON BITES WITH BROCCOLI

2 eggs

1 cup plain dry bread crumbs

¾ teaspoon salt, divided

1 pound skinless salmon fillet, cut into 1-inch pieces

2 cups broccoli florets

1 tablespoon olive oil

Sweet and sour sauce or favorite dipping sauce (optional)

1. Beat eggs in shallow dish. Combine bread crumbs and ½ teaspoon salt in another shallow dish. Dip salmon in eggs, letting excess drip back into dish. Roll in bread crumbs to coat. Place fish on plate; spray with nonstick cooking spray.
2. Preheat air fryer to 390°F. Spray basket with cooking spray.
3. Cook fish in single layer 4 minutes. Turn fish; spray with cooking spray. Cook 3 to 4 minutes or until golden brown. Remove to plate; tent with foil to keep warm.
4. Meanwhile, place broccoli in large bowl; drizzle with oil and toss to coat. Sprinkle with remaining ¼ teaspoon salt.
5. Cook broccoli 6 to 8 minutes or until browned and crisp, shaking halfway through cooking. Serve fish and broccoli with sweet and sour sauce, if desired.

MAKES 5 SERVINGS

VARIATION: Substitute garlic-herb or Italian-seasoned bread crumbs for plain.

CRISP LEMONY BAKED FISH

- **1¼ cups crushed cornflakes**
- **¼ cup grated Parmesan cheese**
- **2 tablespoons minced green onion**
- **⅛ teaspoon black pepper**
- **1 lemon**
- **1 egg**
- **4 haddock fillets (about 4 ounces each)**

1. Combine cornflakes, cheese, green onion and pepper in shallow dish. Grate peel from lemon; stir lemon peel into cornflake mixture. Reserve lemon for serving.
2. Beat egg in another shallow dish. Dip fish in egg, then in cornflake mixture, turning to coat both sides.
3. Preheat air fryer to 380°F. Line basket with parchment paper.
4. Cook fish 8 minutes or until fish begins to flake when tested with fork. Cut reserved lemon into wedges; serve with fish.

MAKES 4 SERVINGS

TERIYAKI SALMON

- ¼ cup dark sesame oil
- Juice of 1 lemon
- ¼ cup soy sauce
- 2 tablespoons packed brown sugar
- 1 clove garlic, minced
- 2 salmon fillets (about 4 ounces each)
- Hot cooked rice (optional)
- Toasted sesame seeds and green onions (optional)

1. Whisk oil, lemon juice, soy sauce, brown sugar and garlic in medium bowl until well blended.
2. Place fish in large resealable food storage bag. Pour marinade over fish; seal bag and turn to coat. Refrigerate at least 2 hours.
3. Preheat air fryer to 390°F. Spray basket with nonstick cooking spray.
4. Cook fish 8 to 10 minutes or until fish begins to flake when tested with fork. Serve with rice; garnish as desired.

MAKES 2 SERVINGS

ROASTED ALMOND TILAPIA

- **2 tilapia or Boston scrod fillets (4 to 6 ounces each)**
- **¼ teaspoon salt**
- **2 teaspoons mustard**
- **¼ cup all-purpose flour**
- **2 tablespoons chopped almonds**
- **Paprika (optional)**
- **Lemon wedges (optional)**

1. Season fish with salt. Spread mustard over fish. Combine flour and almonds in small bowl; sprinkle over fish and press lightly to adhere. Sprinkle with paprika, if desired.
2. Preheat air fryer to 370°F. Line basket with parchment paper.
3. Cook fish 12 to 15 minutes or until opaque in center and fish begins to flake when tested with fork. Serve with lemon wedges, if desired.

MAKES 2 SERVINGS

SIMPLE BAKED COD

- **4 cod fillets (about 6 ounces each)**
- **½ teaspoon salt**
- **¼ teaspoon black pepper**
- **¼ cup (½ stick) butter**
- **1 teaspoon chopped fresh thyme**
- **2 teaspoons grated lemon peel**
- **3 tablespoons chopped fresh parsley**

1. Preheat air fryer to 400°F. Spray basket with nonstick cooking spray.
2. Place fish in basket; sprinkle with salt and pepper.
3. Cook fish 10 to 12 minutes or until fish begins to flake when tested with fork.
4. Meanwhile, melt butter in small saucepan over medium heat. Stir in thyme and lemon peel; cook 1 minute. Remove from heat; stir in parsley. Spoon butter mixture over fish. Serve immediately.

MAKES 4 SERVINGS

DILL-CRUSTED SALMON

- ½ cup panko bread crumbs
- ½ cup finely chopped fresh dill
- 3 tablespoons mayonnaise
- 2 tablespoons olive oil
- 1 teaspoon salt
- ¼ teaspoon red pepper flakes
- 4 salmon fillets (about 5 ounces each)

1. Preheat air fryer to 390°F. Combine panko, dill, mayonnaise, oil, salt and red pepper flakes in medium bowl; mix well.
2. Mound panko mixture evenly over fish, pressing to adhere.
3. Preheat air fryer to 390°F. Line basket with foil or parchment paper; spray with nonstick cooking spray.
4. Cook fish 8 to 12 minutes or until topping is lightly browned and fish begins to flake when tested with fork.

MAKES 4 SERVINGS

ROASTED SESAME FISH

- ¼ cup plus 1 tablespoon soy sauce, divided
- 1 teaspoon dark sesame oil, divided
- 4 skinless tilapia fillets (4 to 5 ounces each)
- 2 teaspoons sesame seeds
- 2 tablespoons sake or dry sherry
- 2 teaspoons grated fresh ginger
- 1 teaspoon sugar
- 1 teaspoon wasabi paste (optional)

1. Preheat air fryer to 375°F. Combine 1 tablespoon soy sauce and ½ teaspoon sesame oil in small bowl; mix well.
2. Place fish in basket. Brush with soy sauce mixture; sprinkle with sesame seeds.
3. Cook fish 8 to 10 minutes or until opaque in center.
4. Meanwhile, whisk remaining ¼ cup soy sauce, ½ teaspoon sesame oil, sake, ginger, sugar and wasabi paste, if desired, in small bowl until well blended. Drizzle over fish.

MAKES 4 SERVINGS

Meatless

CAPRESE PORTOBELLOS

- **2 tablespoons butter**
- **½ teaspoon minced garlic**
- **1 teaspoon dried parsley flakes**
- **4 portobello mushrooms, stems removed**
- **1 cup (4 ounces) shredded mozzarella cheese**
- **1 cup cherry or grape tomatoes, thinly sliced**
- **2 tablespoons thinly sliced fresh basil**
- **Balsamic glaze**

1. Combine butter, garlic and parsley flakes in small microwavable dish; microwave on LOW (30%) 30 seconds or until melted.
2. Preheat air fryer to 390°F. Spray basket with nonstick cooking spray.
3. Brush both sides of mushrooms with butter mixture. Fill each mushroom cap with ¼ cup cheese; top with tomatoes.
4. Cook 5 to 7 minutes or until cheese is melted and lightly browned. Sprinkle with basil; drizzle with balsamic glaze.

MAKES 4 SERVINGS

BLACK BEAN AND RICE STUFFED POBLANO PEPPERS

4 poblano peppers

1 can (about 15 ounces) black beans, rinsed and drained

1 cup cooked brown rice

¾ cup shredded Cheddar cheese or pepper-Jack cheese, divided

⅔ cup chunky salsa

¼ teaspoon salt

1. Cut thin slice from one side of each pepper; remove seeds and membranes. Chop pepper slices; set aside.
2. Preheat air fryer to 380°F. Spray peppers with nonstick cooking spray.
3. Cook peppers 6 to 8 minutes or until skin is slightly softened. Remove to plate. *Reduce temperature of air fryer to 350°F.*
4. Combine beans, rice, ½ cup cheese, salsa, chopped poblano pepper and salt in medium bowl; mix well. Spoon mixture into peppers, mounding in center. Line basket with parchment paper; place filled peppers in basket. (Make sure there is space between peppers for air circulation, or cook in two batches.)
5. Cook filled peppers 6 to 8 minutes or until heated through. Sprinkle with remaining ¼ cup cheese; cook 2 minutes or until cheese is melted.

MAKES 4 SERVINGS

TIP: Use a package of cooked brown rice for the filling to save time.

SPICY EGGPLANT BURGERS

- **1 eggplant (about 1¼ pounds)**
- **2 egg whites**
- **½ cup Italian-style panko bread crumbs**
- **3 tablespoons chipotle mayonnaise or regular mayonnaise**
- **4 whole wheat hamburger buns, warmed**
- **1 cup loosely packed baby spinach**
- **8 thin slices tomato**
- **4 slices pepper Jack cheese**

1. Cut four (½-inch-thick) slices from widest part of eggplant. Beat egg whites in shallow dish. Place panko in another shallow dish.
2. Dip eggplant slices in egg whites; coat with panko, pressing gently to adhere. Spray with nonstick cooking spray.
3. Preheat air fryer to 370°F. Line basket with foil.
4. Cook eggplant in single layer 8 to 10 minutes or until golden brown, turning halfway through cooking.
5. Spread mayonnaise on bottom halves of buns; top with spinach, tomato, eggplant, cheese and tops of buns.

MAKES 4 SERVINGS

FRIED TOFU WITH SESAME DIPPING SAUCE

3 tablespoons soy sauce or tamari

2 tablespoons unseasoned rice vinegar

2 teaspoons sugar

1 teaspoon sesame seeds, toasted*

1 teaspoon dark sesame oil

⅛ teaspoon red pepper flakes

1 package (about 14 ounces) extra firm tofu

¼ cup all-purpose flour

1 egg

1 cup panko bread crumbs

Salt

To toast sesame seeds, cook in small skillet over medium-low heat about 3 minutes or until seeds begin to pop and turn golden, shaking skillet frequently.

1 Whisk soy sauce, vinegar, sugar, sesame seeds, sesame oil and red pepper flakes in small bowl until well blended; set aside.

2 Drain tofu and press between paper towels to remove excess water. Cut crosswise into four slices; cut each slice diagonally into triangles.

3 Place flour in shallow dish. Beat egg in shallow dish. Place panko in another shallow dish.

4 Dip each piece of tofu in flour, turning to lightly coat all sides. Dip in egg, letting excess drip back into bowl. Roll in panko to coat. Season with salt.

5 Preheat air fryer to 390°F. Spray tofu with nonstick cooking spray.

6 Cook tofu in batches 5 to 6 minutes or until golden brown. Serve with sauce for dipping.

MAKES 4 SERVINGS

MEDITERRANEAN GNOCCHI

- **1 package (16 to 17 ounces) shelf-stable gnocchi**
- **2 medium zucchini, quartered lengthwise and cut crosswise into 1-inch pieces**
- **3 medium red onions, halved and cut into ½-inch wedges**
- **1 large red bell pepper, cut into 1-inch pieces**
- **1 pint grape or cherry tomatoes**
- **¼ cup olive oil**
- **2 cloves garlic, minced**
- **1½ teaspoons salt**
- **1 teaspoon dried oregano**
- **1 teaspoon dried rosemary***
- **½ teaspoon black pepper**
- **2 cups baby arugula, divided**
- **½ cup crumbled feta cheese (optional)**

Crush rosemary between your fingers before using to prevent pieces from falling through holes in air fryer basket.

1. Preheat air fryer to 400°F. Combine gnocchi, zucchini, onions, bell pepper and tomatoes in large bowl.
2. Drizzle with oil; sprinkle with garlic, salt, oregano, rosemary and black pepper and toss to coat. Add half of mixture to air fryer basket.
3. Cook 10 minutes or until tomatoes have burst and gnocchi are beginning to brown, shaking halfway through cooking.
4. Stir in 1 cup arugula; close air fryer and let stand 1 minute. (Do not turn on air fryer; residual heat will wilt arugula.) Remove to large bowl; cover to keep warm. Repeat with remaining gnocchi mixture and arugula.
5. Season with additional salt and black pepper; sprinkle with cheese, if desired.

MAKES 4 TO 6 SERVINGS

SOUTHWESTERN FLATBREAD WITH BLACK BEANS AND CORN

- **1 can (about 15 ounces) black beans, rinsed and drained**
- **1 cup frozen corn, thawed**
- **½ cup finely chopped red onion**
- **1 teaspoon olive oil**
- **½ teaspoon salt**
- **¼ cup green chile enchilada sauce**
- **2 oval flatbreads (about 11×7 inches)**
- **2 cups (8 ounces) shredded Monterey Jack cheese**
- **1 avocado, diced**
- **2 tablespoons chopped fresh cilantro**
- **Lime wedges (optional)**

1. Combine beans, corn, onion, oil and salt in medium bowl; mix well.
2. Spread enchilada sauce over flatbreads. Sprinkle with cheese; top with bean mixture.
3. Preheat air fryer to 400°F.
4. Cook flatbreads about 9 minutes or until cheese is melted and crusts are golden brown and crisp.
5. Sprinkle with avocado and cilantro; cut into halves or quarters. Serve with lime wedges, if desired.

MAKES 4 SERVINGS

EGGPLANT PIZZAS

- **1 egg**
- **1 tablespoon water**
- **¾ cup Italian-seasoned dry bread crumbs**
- **1 medium eggplant, cut crosswise into ½-inch slices**
- **½ cup marinara sauce**
- **½ cup (2 ounces) shredded mozzarella cheese**
- **Chopped fresh basil**

1. Beat egg and water in shallow dish. Place bread crumbs in another shallow dish. Dip eggplant slices in egg, letting excess drip back into dish. Coat with bread crumbs, pressing gently to adhere. Spray with nonstick cooking spray.
2. Preheat air fryer to 370°F. Line basket with foil.
3. Cook eggplant in single layer 10 to 12 minutes or until slightly tender and golden brown.
4. Top each eggplant slice with 1 tablespoon marinara sauce and 1 tablespoon cheese. Cook 3 to 5 minutes or until cheese is melted and beginning to brown. Sprinkle with basil just before serving.

MAKES 4 SERVINGS

TIP: Add bell peppers, olives or any other favorite pizza topping to the eggplant with the marinara sauce and cheese.

FRIED TOFU WITH ASIAN VEGETABLES

- **1 pound firm tofu**
- **¼ cup soy sauce, divided**
- **1 cup all-purpose flour**
- **⅛ teaspoon black pepper**
- **1 package (16 ounces) frozen mixed Asian vegetables***
- **3 tablespoons water**
- **1 teaspoon cornstarch**
- **3 tablespoons plum sauce**
- **2 tablespoons lemon juice**
- **2 teaspoons sugar**
- **1 teaspoon minced fresh ginger**
- **⅛ to ¼ teaspoon red pepper flakes**

****Frozen vegetables do not need to be thawed before cooking.***

1. Drain tofu; cut into ¾-inch cubes. Combine tofu and 2 tablespoons soy sauce in shallow dish; stir gently to coat. Let stand 5 minutes. Combine flour and black pepper in another shallow dish. Gently toss tofu cubes, a small amount at a time, with flour mixture to coat. Spray tofu with nonstick cooking spray.

2. Preheat air fryer to 390°F. Cook tofu in batches 3 to 4 minutes or until browned. Remove to plate; tent with foil keep warm.

3. Place frozen vegetables in basket. Cook 3 to 4 minutes or until vegetables are heated through, shaking halfway through cooking.

4. Meanwhile, stir water into cornstarch in small bowl until well blended. Combine cornstarch mixture, remaining 2 tablespoons soy sauce, plum sauce, lemon juice, sugar, ginger and red pepper flakes in medium microwavable bowl; cover and microwave on HIGH 1 minute or until sauce is slightly thickened, stirring after 30 seconds.

5. Spoon vegetables into serving bowl. Top with tofu and sauce; toss gently to blend.

MAKES 6 SERVINGS

BLACK BEAN QUESADILLAS

- **½ cup canned black beans, rinsed and drained**
- **2 green onions, sliced**
- **¼ cup chopped fresh cilantro**
- **½ teaspoon ground cumin**
- **¼ teaspoon salt**
- **4 (8-inch) flour tortillas**
- **¾ cup (3 ounces) shredded Monterey Jack or Mexican blend cheese**
- **Salsa**
- **Sour cream (optional)**

1 Combine beans, green onions, cilantro, cumin and salt in small bowl; mix well.

2 Place two tortillas on work surface; sprinkle each with 3 tablespoons cheese. Spoon bean mixture evenly over cheese; top with remaining cheese and tortillas.

3 Preheat air fryer to 350°F. Spray basket with nonstick cooking spray.

4 Place one quesadilla in basket; spray with cooking spray. Place metal trivet, measuring cup or dinner knife on top of quesadilla to prevent top tortilla from blowing off.

5 Cook 2 minutes; turn and cook 2 minutes or until cheese is melted and quesadillas is lightly browned. Repeat with remaining quesadilla. Cut into quarters; top with salsa and sour cream, if desired.

MAKES 2 SERVINGS

CINNAMON-SUGAR SWEET POTATO FRIES

1 large sweet potato

1 teaspoon butter, melted

1 tablespoon cinnamon-sugar*

To make cinnamon-sugar, combine 1 tablespoon sugar with ½ teaspoon ground cinnamon in small bowl.

1. Peel sweet potato; cut into thin strips. Spray with nonstick cooking spray.
2. Preheat air fryer to 390°F.
3. Cook sweet potato in single layer 15 to 18 minutes or until lightly browned and beginning to crisp, shaking occasionally during cooking. Remove to medium bowl.
4. Add butter and cinnamon-sugar; toss to coat. Serve immediately.

MAKES 2 SERVINGS

THAI BROCCOLI SALAD

- 6 cups fresh broccoli florets (1-inch pieces)
- 1 small red bell pepper, chopped (½-inch pieces)
- 2 tablespoons peanut or vegetable oil
- ¼ teaspoon salt
- 2 tablespoons peanut butter
- 1½ tablespoons hot water
- 1 tablespoon lime juice
- 1 tablespoon packed brown sugar
- 1 tablespoon soy sauce
- 2 teaspoons dark sesame oil
- 1 clove garlic, minced
- ¼ teaspoon red pepper flakes

1. Preheat air fryer to 360°F.
2. Combine broccoli and bell pepper in large bowl. Drizzle with peanut oil and sprinkle with salt; toss to coat.
3. Cook vegetables 15 minutes or until crisp-tender, shaking twice during cooking.
4. Meanwhile, whisk peanut butter, water, lime juice, brown sugar, soy sauce, sesame oil, garlic and red pepper flakes in large bowl until smooth and well blended.
5. Add vegetables to peanut butter mixture; toss to coat. Serve warm or at room temperature.

MAKES 4 TO 6 SERVINGS

MEXICAN CORN RIBS

2 ears corn

¼ cup (½ stick) butter, softened

½ teaspoon chili powder

¼ teaspoon garlic powder

¼ teaspoon black pepper

¼ cup mayonnaise

2 teaspoons lime juice

1 teaspoon hot pepper sauce

2 tablespoons cotija or feta cheese

1 tablespoon chopped fresh cilantro

1 Husk corn and remove silk. Rinse and dry corn. Use large knife to cut ears of corn in half horizontally, then cut each half lengthwise into quarters to create four "ribs."

2 Combine butter, chili powder, garlic powder and black pepper in small bowl; mix well. Spread mixture over corn.

3 Preheat air fryer to 390°F. Line basket with parchment paper.

4 Cook corn 12 to 14 minutes or until charred, turning halfway through cooking. Remove to plate.

5 Meanwhile, combine mayonnaise, lime juice and hot pepper sauce in small bowl; mix well. Brush over hot corn; sprinkle with cheese and cilantro.

MAKES 4 SERVINGS

BROWN SUGAR–BACON BRUSSELS SPROUTS

- **1 pound Brussels sprouts**
- **2 slices bacon, cut into ½-inch pieces**
- **2 teaspoons packed brown sugar**
- **Salt and black pepper**

1. Trim ends from Brussels sprouts; cut in half lengthwise.
2. Preheat air fryer to 390°F. Combine Brussels sprouts, bacon and brown sugar in large bowl; mix well.
3. Cook Brussels sprouts 15 to 18 minutes or until golden brown, shaking occasionally during cooking. Season with salt and pepper.

MAKES 4 SERVINGS

TACO-ROASTED CAULIFLOWER

- **1 medium cauliflower (about 2 pounds), cut into florets**
- **2 tablespoons vegetable oil**
- **1 package (1 ounce) taco seasoning mix**

1. Preheat air fryer to 370°F.
2. Place cauliflower in large bowl. Drizzle with oil and sprinkle with seasoning mix; toss to coat.
3. Cook cauliflower 20 to 25 minutes or until tender and lightly browned, shaking twice during cooking.*

**Cooking the entire cauliflower in one batch will result in tender cauliflower that is less crisp. For crisper cauliflower, cook in single layer in several batches; reduce cooking time to 15 minutes and shake halfway through cooking.*

MAKES 4 TO 6 SERVINGS

GARLIC AIR-FRIED FRIES

- **2 large russet potatoes, peeled and cut into matchstick strips**
- **1 tablespoon plus 2 teaspoons olive oil, divided**
- **1½ teaspoons minced garlic**
- **½ teaspoon salt**
- **½ teaspoon dried parsley flakes**
- **¼ teaspoon black pepper**
- **Blue cheese dressing, ranch dressing and/or ketchup (optional)**

1. Combine potatoes and 2 teaspoons oil in medium bowl; toss to coat.
2. Preheat air fryer to 390°F. Line basket with parchment paper.
3. Cook potatoes in batches 8 to 10 minutes or until golden brown and crisp, shaking occasionally during cooking.
4. Meanwhile, combine remaining 1 tablespoon oil, garlic, salt, parsley flakes and pepper in medium bowl; mix well.
5. Add warm fries to garlic mixture; toss to coat. Serve immediately with desired sauces.

MAKES 4 SERVINGS

ROASTED BALSAMIC ASPARAGUS

- **1 pound fresh asparagus**
- **1 tablespoon olive oil**
- **½ teaspoon salt**
- **¼ teaspoon black pepper**
- **1 tablespoon balsamic glaze***
- **¼ cup shredded or grated Parmesan cheese**
- **Grated lemon peel (optional)**

Balsamic glaze can be found in the condiment section of the supermarket, or it can be prepared by simmering 2 tablespoons balsamic vinegar until reduced by about half.

1. Preheat air fryer to 400°F.
2. Place asparagus in shalllow dish. Drizzle with oil and season with salt and pepper; roll spears to coat.
3. Cook asparagus in single layer 6 to 8 minutes or until tender and beginning to brown, shaking halfway through cooking. Transfer to serving plate.
4. Drizzle with balsamic glaze; roll again with tongs to coat. Sprinkle with cheese; garnish with lemon peel.

MAKES 4 SERVINGS

AIR-FRIED CAULIFLOWER FLORETS

- **1 head cauliflower**
- **1 tablespoon olive oil**
- **3 tablespoons grated Parmesan cheese**
- **2 tablespoons panko bread crumbs**
- **1 tablespoon chopped fresh parsley**
- **½ teaspoon salt**
- **¼ teaspoon black pepper**

1. Cut cauliflower into florets. Place in large bowl; drizzle with oil. Sprinkle with cheese, panko, parsley, salt and pepper; toss to coat.
2. Preheat air fryer to 390°F. Spray basket with nonstick cooking spray.
3. Cook cauliflower in batches 12 to 15 minutes or until lightly browned, shaking every 5 minutes.

MAKES 4 SERVINGS

SWEET POTATO FRIES

- **2 sweet potatoes, peeled and sliced**
- **1 tablespoon olive oil**
- **¼ teaspoon coarse salt**
- **¼ teaspoon black pepper**

1 Combine potatoes, oil, salt and pepper in medium bowl; toss to coat.

2 Preheat air fryer to 390°F. Spray basket with nonstick cooking spray.

3 Cook sweet potatoes in batches 10 to 12 minutes or until lightly browned, shaking occasionally during cooking.

MAKES 2 SERVINGS

HERBED CREMINI MUSHROOMS

- **1 pound cremini mushrooms, halved or quartered if large**
- **½ cup sliced shallots**
- **1 tablespoon olive oil**
- **¾ teaspoon salt**
- **½ teaspoon dried rosemary, crushed***
- **¼ teaspoon black pepper**
- **Fresh rosemary sprigs (optional)**

****Crush rosemary between your fingers before using to prevent pieces from falling through holes in air fryer basket.***

1. Preheat air fryer to 370°F.
2. Combine mushrooms and shallots in medium bowl. Drizzle with oil; sprinkle with salt, dried rosemary and pepper and toss to coat.
3. Cook mushrooms 8 to 10 minutes or until tender and lightly browned, shaking twice during cooking. Garnish with fresh rosemary.

MAKES 4 SERVINGS

CINNAMON HONEY GLAZED CARROT CHIPS

- ¼ **cup honey**
- **2 tablespoons butter**
- **1 teaspoon ground cinnamon**
- ½ **teaspoon ground nutmeg**
- **Pinch of salt**
- **1 package (16 ounces) carrot chips or baby carrots**

1. Combine honey and butter in medium microwavable bowl; microwave on HIGH 30 seconds or until melted. Add cinnamon, nutmeg and salt; stir until blended.
2. Add carrots to honey mixture; stir to coat.
3. Preheat air fryer to 390°F. Line basket with parchment paper.
4. Cook carrots in batches 12 to 15 minutes or until slightly tender and browned, shaking halfway through cooking.

MAKES 6 SERVINGS

ONION-SEASONED POTATOES

2 pounds russet potatoes, cut into 1-inch pieces

2 tablespoons olive oil

1 package (1 ounce) onion soup mix

1. Preheat air fryer to 360°F.
2. Place potatoes in medium bowl. Drizzle with oil and sprinkle with soup mix; toss to coat.
3. Cook potatoes in batches about 22 minutes or until tender and golden brown, shaking and spraying with olive oil cooking spray halfway through cooking.

MAKES 4 SERVINGS

NOTE: If your air fryer basket has large holes, pieces from the soup mix may fall through during cooking and shaking. To prevent this, line your air fryer basket with parchment paper or foil before cooking.

SAVORY GARLIC MUSHROOMS

- **1 pound mushrooms, cut into thick slices**
- **2 tablespoons olive oil**
- **1 teaspoon garlic powder**
- **1 teaspoon Italian seasoning**
- **½ teaspoon salt**
- **¼ teaspoon black pepper**

1. Preheat air fryer to 370°F.
2. Combine mushrooms, oil, garlic powder, Italian seasoning, salt and pepper in large bowl; toss to coat.
3. Cook mushrooms 12 to 15 minutes or until tender and browned, shaking occasionally during cooking.

MAKES 4 SERVINGS

BUTTERNUT SQUASH FRIES

- ½ **teaspoon garlic powder**
- ¼ **teaspoon salt**
- ¼ **teaspoon ground red pepper**
- 1 **butternut squash (about 2½ pounds), peeled, seeded and cut into thin slices about 2 inches long**
- 2 **teaspoons vegetable oil**

1. Preheat air fryer to 390°F. Combine garlic powder, salt and red pepper in small bowl; mix well.
2. Place squash in large bowl. Drizzle with oil and sprinkle with seasoning mixture; toss to coat.
3. Cook squash in batches 16 to 18 minutes or until tender and browned, shaking halfway through cooking.

MAKES 4 SERVINGS

SWEET AND SPICY SWEET POTATO FRIES

- **2 pounds sweet potatoes, peeled and cut into ½-inch sticks**
- **2 tablespoons cornstarch**
- **2 tablespoons vegetable oil**
- **2 tablespoons taco seasoning mix**
- **1 teaspoon packed brown sugar**
- **¼ teaspoon salt**
- **Chipotle Lime Sauce (optional, recipe follows)**

1. Preheat air fryer to 360°F.
2. Combine sweet potatoes and cornstarch in large bowl; toss to coat. Drizzle with oil; toss to coat. Sprinkle with taco seasoning mix, brown sugar and salt, stir until evenly coated.
3. Cook sweet potatoes in batches about 20 minutes or until lightly browned and crisp, shaking halfway through cooking.
4. Meanwhile, prepare Chipotle Lime Sauce, if desired. Serve with sweet potatoes.

MAKES 4 SERVINGS

CHIPOTLE LIME SAUCE: Combine 1 cup sour cream, 1 tablespoon lime juice and 1 teaspoon chipotle chili powder in small bowl; mix well.

GARLIC ROASTED OLIVES AND TOMATOES

1 cup assorted olives, pitted
1 cup grape tomatoes, halved
4 cloves garlic, sliced
1 tablespoon olive oil
1 tablespoon herbes de Provence

1. Preheat air fryer to 370°F.
2. Pat olives dry with paper towels. Combine olives, tomatoes, garlic and oil in small bowl. Stir in herbes de Provence; mix well.
3. Spread olive mixture in basket. Cook 5 to 7 minutes or until tomatoes are browned and blistered, shaking occasionally during cooking.

MAKES ABOUT 2 CUPS

SERVING SUGGESTION: Serve with toasted bread as an appetizer, or toss with hot cooked pasta for a main dish.

AIR-ROASTED SWEET POTATOES

- **2 sweet potatoes, peeled and cut into thin slices or spiral slices**
- **1 tablespoon olive oil**
- **¼ teaspoon salt**
- **⅛ teaspoon black pepper**
- **¼ cup grated Parmesan cheese (optional)**

1. Preheat air fryer to 330°F.
2. Combine sweet potatoes and oil in medium bowl; toss to coat. Season with salt and pepper.
3. Cook sweet potatoes in batches 20 to 22 minutes, shaking halfway through cooking. Sprinkle with cheese, if desired.

MAKES 4 SERVINGS

AIR-FRIED CORN ON THE COB

- **2 teaspoons butter, melted**
- **1 teaspoon chopped fresh parsley**
- **¼ teaspoon salt**
- **¼ teaspoon black pepper**
- **2 ears corn, husks and silks removed**
- **Grated Parmesan cheese (optional)**

1 Combine butter, parsley, salt and pepper in small bowl; mix well.

2 Preheat air fryer to 390°F. Brush corn with butter mixture. Wrap each ear of corn in foil.*

3 Cook corn 6 to 8 minutes, turning halfway through cooking. Sprinkle with cheese, if desired.

**If your air fryer basket is too small to fit whole ears of corn, break them in half to fit.*

MAKES 2 SERVINGS

Index

Index

Index

Index

METRIC CONVERSION CHART

VOLUME MEASUREMENTS (dry)

1/8 teaspoon = 0.5 mL
1/4 teaspoon = 1 mL
1/2 teaspoon = 2 mL
3/4 teaspoon = 4 mL
1 teaspoon = 5 mL
1 tablespoon = 15 mL
2 tablespoons = 30 mL
1/4 cup = 60 mL
1/3 cup = 75 mL
1/2 cup = 125 mL
2/3 cup = 150 mL
3/4 cup = 175 mL
1 cup = 250 mL
2 cups = 1 pint = 500 mL
3 cups = 750 mL
4 cups = 1 quart = 1 L

VOLUME MEASUREMENTS (fluid)

1 fluid ounce (2 tablespoons) = 30 mL
4 fluid ounces (1/2 cup) = 125 mL
8 fluid ounces (1 cup) = 250 mL
12 fluid ounces (1 1/2 cups) = 375 mL
16 fluid ounces (2 cups) = 500 mL

WEIGHTS (mass)

1/2 ounce = 15 g
1 ounce = 30 g
3 ounces = 90 g
4 ounces = 120 g
8 ounces = 225 g
10 ounces = 285 g
12 ounces = 360 g
16 ounces = 1 pound = 450 g

DIMENSIONS

1/16 inch = 2 mm
1/8 inch = 3 mm
1/4 inch = 6 mm
1/2 inch = 1.5 cm
3/4 inch = 2 cm
1 inch = 2.5 cm

OVEN TEMPERATURES

250°F = 120°C
275°F = 140°C
300°F = 150°C
325°F = 160°C
350°F = 180°C
375°F = 190°C
400°F = 200°C
425°F = 220°C
450°F = 230°C

BAKING PAN SIZES

Utensil	Size in Inches/Quarts	Metric Volume	Size in Centimeters
Baking or Cake Pan (square or rectangular)	8×8×2	2 L	20×20×5
	9×9×2	2.5 L	23×23×5
	12×8×2	3 L	30×20×5
	13×9×2	3.5 L	33×23×5
Loaf Pan	8×4×3	1.5 L	20×10×7
	9×5×3	2 L	23×13×7
Round Layer Cake Pan	8×1½	1.2 L	20×4
	9×1½	1.5 L	23×4
Pie Plate	8×1¼	750 mL	20×3
	9×1¼	1 L	23×3
Baking Dish or Casserole	1 quart	1 L	—
	1½ quart	1.5 L	—
	2 quart	2 L	—